SHALE BINGS

Ian Macartney is a writer who can be found online at ianmacartney. scot, but for how much longer?

CONTENTS

ISBN: 978-1-916938-05-2

Cover designed by Aaron Kent

Edited and Typeset by Aaron Kent

Broken Sleep Books Ltd
PO BOX 102
Llandysul
SA44 9BG

Shale Bings

Ian Macartney

Broken Sleep Books

i.m. Rowie.

THE RETURN

for Jordan

I brought it back. What weren't we waiting for? You winked like a kind of clear moon, tarot too hard to read. Invoked stricture, charts of the flaming, the womb. And I don't have a sensibility to share – I care less about stars than smiles, the close-up of Lover's face, you know? We share that, the beach a cheaper ring, toy-ruby and rusted nail, two-strung curl the tunnel of the train like woods a hollow warping leaves so light, symmetry or parallax from the pines many lines so threads of silver, rust, the ring morning-stretched as Lover intended! I follow mops of green – I follow the way you face day in moon, Pictland, the world a wood. Miss your tongue. Escape to where the scene cannot reach, slope and track and reverse slope, leaves envisioned in grass' hair ruffled by the winds like some faint hand, a stray tap and carry and flow on ponds painted by flowers gestu-reflecting come summer, purple or amber or teal. To see a spot and think, I love you. Tomato seeds. Give me totem, give me pleasure, give me permission, just because, ecstatic trots calmed by the walk-weary weight of Inverness, her firm press to suitcase, the warm face of Three Graces –

Faith! Chance! Memory!

Inverness to Linlithgow, July 2020 (12th)

MUIRAVONSIDE, JULY 2020 (20TH)

for Caoilte

under the canal
were the brightest lengths of wood
If fell then of pulleys
Those oak ropes Skin certain
and chitinous-bronze
There was the moss wall
of childhood's kingdom
You know Who would walk back
to the forest Woods a child
could only reach from the family car
Labradors in firm tow
Stupid with happy Splashing
over the wilder river Pure Porous
soil Some stones Noon-glazed
Tap that which is raw muscle Tree bough

pulp up O aqueduct Brick pale as cloud
You know more than i could ever dream
Gantries over stone Knuckles in the leafed
smell Dry with life like earth
unpacked Loose A forest to ramble in
multiple directions envisioned when 12
Kettlestoun mains Wandered with ewan
Cakes of greenery by the flooded mine
I remembered i did not have to grow up
or be zealous about age So we
walked and played and felt good
in that bud of love which blooms

despite my butterflied judgement
Endless topaz bubble popped
off the spirit-level (home unbuilt
during this dull intermediate yawning)
like perfection Like a blood blister Pus
Nectary I learned from my ex *You want*
every interaction to be fluid

and Intrusive thought are symbols of ocd
The bridge was also very very scary
Thumb to finger's pad A coin of ash
below Smudged grey Lipsticked
There was the froth of an estuary gone
cartographic The brown in old maps
The rainbow was also a bough
A staggering double Bismuth moon
fully waned in the bright day
The beautiful scent of warm rain
It was a blessing for that
and a furious sign of forgiveness
Strident as lightning
Anti-diluvian

DANDELION SEED, TRAMPOLINE, AUGUST 2014 (1ST)

At first I thought it *Opiliones*

until it was a seed.
Globed skeletal information.

That spark of philosophy
flew to my torso, hugged

    then humbled
me,

the thought gone. I left to grow
towards some other home.

THE SNAILS MOVE OUT

Rain made the spiral houses
part away from each other
on gelatinous railways.
A town disbanded.

They migrated
across pavements with
staircases on their backs,

slugging through pools of their own body,
Golden Ratios crushed by feet
from above.

Living-rooms flooded in
a tear-drop apocalypse.
Fibonacci caved –

the mangled fluid turned clay-red.
The others had to go
before the eels they built their houses on
swam away in the flying water.

BEAUTIFUL MOTH CAPTURED IN GLASS
THEN RELEASED!!!!!!!!!!!!!

I

a)

Used [i]non-
places[/i] 2
capture the flow
of ur response
battering smol air
wi a long see
-thru knot

b)

Took pictures
wowed via glass
in ur stretch of space
(capsule-object) coz
ur ammonitic front
turned wi cup 2 face
the metal eye in my blind hand

c)

Window opened 2 far
as if a door
2 sell the light from
in the morning

this night &
u flew to the concrete
side of the sill

II

Albino barked wi lichen fans

SLOPE OF SOIL, LINLITHGOW, OCTOBER 2020 (18TH)

weeding. spangles of hair in primordial soup.

kneading. cocoa dough boot-smoothed.

firmer by the firmament of rocks.

dangling flowing islands
tailed, not ornaments,
verdant obliquity

aether's
aureity, clanging

copper, feathery, bird bones,
autumnal pleasance

fork bell against the pebble-chine,
soil suckered to the cellular – well, knot,
you know, but like surgery, says neighbour, retired doctor

that very scene in the blockbuster,
the rising plateau,
green gone comet

the shock of brighter the deeper
heavier then satisfying, pull-up,
stomach on end to weigh better,
corkscrew seppuku, wait

unthinking cellular whip,
specimen raised for the compartment,
the elsewhere dumped elsewhere

grey-caked
drain for the world-dish,
the lateral value of roots, arborising moon, reeling vein,
blind muchness (mulch, duh)

headphone wire to the green cup at air's ear.
so too my bulb, steve reich's meditation. even
my headache was part of the complex percussion
of mister steve life. it is minecraft night.

try for the root note.
doodle through soil.

no city nor jungle stands over
the four toddler-thumb holes of a fork,
an iron rib

dead leaf preserved,
quartz-ish

ginger dreamcatchers,
bronze, so deep the vein

flecks of whiter powder, unearthed,
chalk or glistening, likely neither

then a pearlescent root
began to move. a shock – a worm – living !
end milk, undead, the trail of exertion
vulnerable, new

SLUG IN SINK

I was in the sink, all the browns and greens of a tree. Flat black cardboard escorted me out.

From the vegetable gardens to the fruit I curled and thinned and fattened into an alphabet.

Near a leaf I dived into the world gracing his hand with soft discovery, a toddler's thumb.

BLACKBERRIES, OUT HERE

for Lisa Boyle

Plants grow boisterous
thorns in isolation. Away from Man
in the Garden of Silence
the crunch of twig scared only

me. To find him writing is worse than thinking
me naked – pen on paper. The first train
was an anticipated dread that scared
no tree but I, hands clasped

to each hot ear until he could hear only
my palm line. Disappointed leaves.
Train-brought breeze eventually
anticipated a trickle of windchimes

for now blackberries grew on the fence
next to my railway, out of reach, though
like all mothers the robin (tumble of pollen
in the whimsy of wind) succeeded. Which was good.

*

When you go to the riverbed of wet leaves
swotted, aghast, off branches via secret tree,
unsuccessful, you must look for where the half-hearted

burn began. When we find the low stone tunnel
under moss and soil, notice how above
the long source they, alone, were, always.

Linlithgow, October 2015 (6th)

WHILE EATING PRINGLES (OR, WORLD MESSAGE)

– whisper, regardless, to (

poppy in chorus of green wheat
rain-speckled whisker | threading
-coloured chandelier | playpark
tree hair monocombed along honey
-light | shadow taller than rainbow
trunk anchor-horizon | clouded
assurance paint-peach soap
bubble adrift whirl-motion
-cream-paint-tendril-whatever O
blush grey edge vacuum-flush
|| streetlight dawn super-low orb
|| earliest train under
silver gates // Go

) type my message on coal
one swipe from the worst
websites. Clouds conjugate

spaceships above, salt diamonds
clicked to place only my soft
pink parabola, ever-tasting,

in silence –

Springfield, Linlithgow, August 2014 (24th)

SHALE BINGS

for Andrew, Calhan, Daniel, Ewan, Harry, Kyle

Dragged from rock and pieced earth
we plateaued to an adolescent mountain.

Looking to oilseed seas
beside fields the dull green of cloud
we breathed in West Lothian, the three bridges

layering a metal history
on shrouded water, newest
white, cabled like angel wings,

for *this is the world's centre for shale
once*. Paths snaked down, imprinted,
the erosion of ancient waves on our version of Mars,

the planet thought of by children.
Swimming through nettles at our waists
and lichen coral on the black rock of old trees

we scaled routes made difficult
by easier machinery, each footstep
a tide of lost-shaped shells, trainers red

when we reached the top.
Us, a haggle of teenagers discovering
bathtubs for baptism, their emerald water,

empty bottles like crystal caskets,
dirt-lanterned, the brick layout of ruined
quarry shrines wrecked by distant wind. A wall of sky

approaches, the presence of drizzle
imminent. Below, in a sunken path of maze,
we wandered in crop fields, our breezed malachite marine,

soil set like a farm gate lock,
tire tracks preceding the wider road.

Winchburgh, May 2016 (10th)

EARLY MORNING, SHROPSHIRE, FEBRUARY 2016 (20TH)

for Allie, Apollo, Eira, Gaia, Jack, Kajol, Lydia, Mag, Maud,
Mikaela, Reem, Riona, Sasha, Tait

The lake is still, frozen time
underneath. Green smoke
rises from sheds cushioned

in ivy. I am always walking.
The road paces like darkness
looking for its emerald – in torch

-white all walls become lakes.
I am looking for the door
of light on my retina

because I blinked at the sky
once, stars like snow on the edge
of every glazed expression,

the tilt's moon titled
"A Mother's Head".

SLATER

Sheets of metal shift
  (long, the sea floor).
From the ocean you rose
  as king of fallen trees,
prehistoric, boards
  chewed to the resin.
"Permanent". Boat-builder,
  butcher-boy, carcass
off Theseus' ship, empires
  in red... you have seen
it all, bug, futurist
  sower, fourteen
bits – living pendant –
  our gaunt tenant.

SNAIL CLIMBS

Scared static on a sliced leaf the snail's
back-borne spiral cog spluttered, started

sudden, slid to
encrusted wood,
body a full mouth
kissing the ground
scaled anticlockwise
towards leaf-lit tops,
other shells above
beset in grooves
like pale pearls.

I grip pliers. Careless ape. I could cut its opal fruit with ease.

Still. We gaze upward, sweetened mouths fated forever open.

LINLITHGOW TO GLASGOW QUEEN STREET, MAY 2022 (6TH)

for Shaw

everyone is secretly smiling
at the amazing dog
lying panting (whining)
under the seat in front

of the amazing dog's
tourist couple (winning) &

are we not all strangers
who will not say this
to know so well in

loving them (dog) together
we smile towards each other

more
only MIRACLE (we message
my friend) TRAIN MIRACLE

WATERING

four days alone
in the home (farmhouse
renovated Once) Grandparents
said plants would be watered
They crisp Dogbowl's rain
gone sour Yellowing emerald
Garage key gone Could not
use full the water Technology curled
and spooled Collected
from a wounded nozzle
Therapeutic motion Dribbled
to a can Bloodletting Dropped
like spittle Connection
to the source Pacifier The can
heavy like holding
"my child" Palm on bottom
as she throws up Spilled
tubes Bloated artery
Clear electricity O
i left the lights on
Room in a dark house
The sky drains Lamps pop
by the lawn full
of clover White
bunches Metropolis
of pollen So close
So vibrant Somehow
living in four-day heat

Stone pots small temples
to yellowing gods
Golden patches in the grass
Maroon leaves bowed Touching
the ground Weeping branch
Not a vegetative crunch More a plea
Red trumpets paled out
Scented shells laid for snails
Their platter glided off the stalk (it was the longest line
of the plant) Dry
leaflitter like flayed lips
pleading A suck of wet soil Please I
tickle the ground Treacle leaves
the can Miracles Bangle
of cold blood round my wrist
Do i imagine rebirth Dark
desert of moisture Gate-spark Whispers
in a sprinkle of water through
ship-shaped green plastic
that does hee-haw The old
sit still twiddling thumbs
to extinction Water flows
in Out Return
to the soil The roots Need
to drink a glass of water
A headache is thundering
I feel it halve the skull I need
to go in Get a glass
of water Goodbye world
i tried to save We met

a ball of root Made our own
veins Called it blood
Now a country has lost Its heads
of power roll And something dark
will soon come Maybe
some will survive Maybe
we harvest warmth Maybe
we make our own hell

Linlithgow, July 2018 (11th)

WALKING ON SWINGS

for Becky

Wobbling above wet grass
on a plastic hoverboard rope-taut

I look to constellations
for consolation. Orion's Belt seeks

its stopped place past the first half
of a question mark, jumping from

these plates children leap off
in tandem to friendlier pendulums

and I yearn for what is lost
when moving from years of agony

so comfortable into sometime
unknown. When a friend finds me

with his phone-light I clutch his back,
shoeless, into the warmer house party

and wonder if this time and more
will become bone-white spots

                                        tracing maps of the sky

Bathgate, February 2016 (12th)

MUIRAVONSIDE, JANUARY 2015 (2ND)

Moon! Oval opal cloud
above the amber resin
seeping from the forge

a divine blush bronzing
cotton-stalks, the taut
sleeping flowers – you

are the cove of a close road,
a long stretch downhill
to the river-place

of dancing dogs, your
rain in blossom when
we accomplish our return!

WALKING, THEN, SLIDING ACROSS ICE

Stars spot the sky like God's acne
(His problem, I need to remember,

specks of half-hydrogen celestial
crumbs not brushed off, puckered,

O to build things). The dark side
rests orb-like on its slice of moon,

black coin pressed to light,
glistening outline guiltless

as an undone zip snake-esque
in the unclean screen's reflection,

the car window, the sparkling
field, fallen frost like feathers.

We walk through streets silent
in stone's shade. It's morning,

technically, pavement petrified or shrouded
in grey clay – my soleless shoes slide easy

over strange roads we walked past
in the day, purgatorial as cloud, but

now we are adults, apparently,
so the body goes slack, keeps flat in its headway without
    falling over, no, not even once, I promise nothing else

Linlithgow, January 2017 (2nd)

ACKNOWLEDGEMENTS

beautiful moth captured in glass then released!!!!!!!!!!!! / was first published by *Ex/Post* in 2020

The Snails Move Out / was first published on the Poetry Society website in 2015

While Eating Pringles (or, World Message) / was first published by *unpopular zine* in 2021

Shale Bings / premiered on BBC Radio Scotland in 2019

Snail Climbs / was first published by *Leopard Arts* in 2020

Linlithgow to Glasgow Queen Street, May 2022 (6th) / was first published by Good Press' *The Paper* in 2022

Watering / was first published by *Icarus* in 2019

Walking on Swings / was first published by *Scoot Around* in 2019

Walking, Then, Sliding Across Ice / was first published by *Weavers* in 2022

LAY OUT YOUR UNREST

www.ingramcontent.com/pod-product-compliance
Lightning Source LLC
Chambersburg PA
CBHW051741040426
42447CB00008B/1248